First
Facts®

Get To Know
Reptiles

Get to Know

GECKOS

WITHDRAWN

by Flora Brett

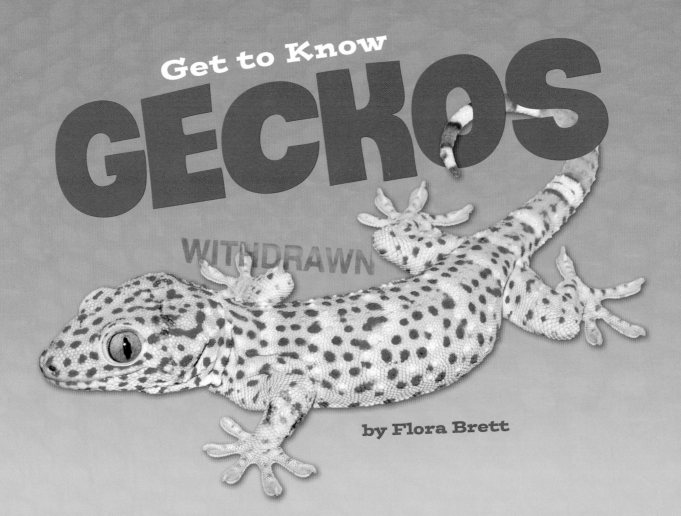

CAPSTONE PRESS
a capstone imprint

First Facts are published by Capstone Press,
1710 Roe Crest Drive, North Mankato, Minnesota 56003
www.capstonepub.com

Library of Congress Cataloging-in-Publication Data
Brett, Flora, author.
Get to know geckos / by Flora Brett.
    pages cm.—(First facts. Get to know reptiles)
Summary: "Discusses geckos, including their physical features, habitat, range,
diet, and life cycle."—Provided by publisher.
Audience: Ages 6–9.
Audience: K to grade 3.
Includes bibliographical references and index.
ISBN 978-1-4914-2060-7 (library binding)
ISBN 978-1-4914-2244-1 (pbk.)
ISBN 978-1-4914-2266-3 (ebook PDF)
1. Geckos—Juvenile literature. I. Title.
QL666.L245B74 2015
597.95'2—dc23
                    2014023857

Editorial Credits
Nikki Bruno Clapper, editor; Cynthia Akiyoshi, designer; Svetlana
    Zhurkin, media researcher; Katy LaVigne, production specialist

Photo Credits
Dreamstime: Pawel Opaska, 11; FLPA: Chris Mattison, 15 (bottom); Minden
Pictures: NPL/Robert Valentic, 17; Newscom: Photoshot/NHPA/Thomas
Kitchin & Victoria Hurst, 21; Shutterstock: Bronwyn Photo, 20, Cathy Keifer,
back cover, 13, Dean Pennala, 5, kitsana, cover, 1, 2, 24, Melissa Brandes, 9
(bottom), Robyn Mackenzie, 6, Ryan M. Bolton, 7, smishonja, 19, Tatiana
Yakovleva (background), cover and throughout

Printed in the United States of America in North Mankato, Minnesota.
092014   008482CGS15

Table of Contents

Loud Lizards

Chirp! Bark! Squeak! Click! Geckos make all these sounds. The lizards make noise to defend themselves from **predators**.

Geckos and other lizards are **reptiles**. Reptiles are **cold-blooded** animals. They cannot make their own body heat.

More than 1,000 **species** of geckos live around the world. They make up about 25 percent of all lizards.

predator—an animal that hunts other animals for food

reptile—a cold-blooded animal that breathes air and has a backbone; most reptiles have scales

cold-blooded—having a body temperature that changes with the surrounding temperature

species—a group of animals with similar features

Scales, Tails, and Toes

A gecko's colorful body is covered with scales. Geckos have large heads with big eyes. Most geckos are less than 12 inches (30 centimeters) long.

A gecko's tail can break off if a predator grabs it. The tail twitches even after it falls off! In a few months, the tail grows back.

Geckos have pads on the bottoms of their feet. Tiny hairs on the pads grab on to surfaces. Geckos can run across a ceiling without falling!

lined day gecko

Fact:

Geckos have see-through eyelids. They lick the eye area to keep their eyelids clean.

Warm Around the World

Geckos live on every continent except Antarctica. Australia has more than 100 kinds of geckos. Geckos live in warm places. These lizards spend a lot of time in the sun. Their bodies soak up heat from their surroundings.

A few kinds of geckos live in the United States. Banded geckos are found in the Southwest. The leaf-toed gecko lives in California. Hawaii has many kinds of geckos.

Fact:
The tokay gecko from Southeast Asia is the largest gecko. It grows about 14 inches (36 cm) long.

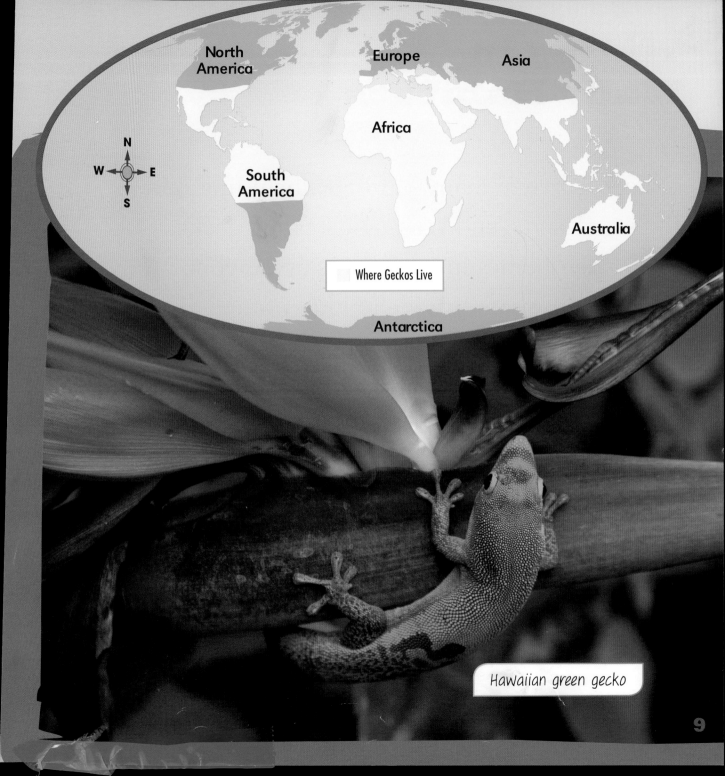

North America

Europe

Asia

Africa

South America

Australia

Where Geckos Live

Antarctica

N
W · E
S

Hawaiian green gecko

Hiding in Many Habitats

Geckos live in many habitats, including rain forests, deserts, and grasslands. Some geckos make their homes in mountains or canyons.

Geckos use camouflage to hide from predators. They blend in with leaves, branches, rocks, and sand. The leaf-tailed gecko lives in trees. The banded gecko hides in sand dunes.

Most geckos are nocturnal. They rest during the day and look for food at night.

Fact:

A gecko called the Jaragua lizard is the smallest lizard in the world. It can fit on a dime.

leaf-tailed gecko
camouflaged on branch

habitat—the natural place and conditions in which a plant or animal lives

camouflage—a pattern or color on an animal's skin that helps it blend in with the things around it

nocturnal—active at night and resting during the day

Finding Food

What kind of **prey** do geckos look for at night? Mainly they eat insects and spiders. Many people in the Philippines and Central America like having geckos in their homes. Geckos keep the bugs away!

Some large geckos eat smaller geckos or small **mammals** such as mice. A few geckos eat fruit. The forest gecko in New Zealand eats nectar from flowers.

prey—an animal hunted by another animal for food

mammal—a warm-blooded animal that breathes air; mammals have hair or fur; female mammals feed milk to their young

Fact:

Some geckos store fat in their tails. The fat helps them stay alive when they cannot find food.

leopard gecko
hunting a fly

Extra-Special Eggs

Most female geckos **mate** with males and then lay eggs. Female geckos usually lay two soft, white eggs at a time. The shells harden and protect the babies from wind and rain. Some geckos lay 10 sets of eggs each year.

Mother geckos lay their eggs under leaves or bark. The eggs hatch after about two months. Gecko **hatchlings** use a tooth called an egg tooth to escape from their eggs.

Fact:

A few gecko species do not lay eggs. Instead they give birth to live young.

mate—to join with another to produce young

hatchling—a young animal that has just come out of its egg

Gecko Life Cycle
A gecko hatches and becomes an adult. Then it mates and has its own babies.

Growing Up Gecko

Young geckos look like small adults. They live on their own as soon as they hatch. They hunt for food right away. By age 2 most geckos can mate and produce young.

Geckos **molt** as they grow. The skin breaks open at the animal's head and falls off down its back.

molt—to shed an outer layer of skin

old skin

tesselated gecko molting

Fact:

Some geckos eat the
skin they shed.

Threats to Geckos

Geckos have many predators. Other lizards, snakes, frogs, foxes, birds, and crocodiles hunt geckos. Spiders may eat the smallest geckos.

People are the biggest danger to geckos. Sometimes people catch wild geckos and sell them as pets. This practice is especially harmful to rare gecko species. People also **breed** geckos for use as pets. It is better to buy these geckos.

People clear land to build towns and cities. This practice destroys gecko habitats.

breed—to mate and raise a certain kind of animal

European roller
eating a gecko

Pet Geckos

Do you think you might want a pet gecko? Most geckos are easy to keep as pets. Leopard geckos make especially good pets. Adult leopard geckos do not even need to be fed every day. These geckos can live for up to 20 years.

Fact:
In the wild leopard geckos eat scorpions. These geckos can survive scorpion stings.

Amazing but True!

Flying geckos don't really fly, but they can glide from tree to tree! They have small skin flaps on their heads and sides. These flaps catch air like parachutes. The geckos' flat tails also help them glide. Gliding helps the geckos escape from predators.

Glossary

breed (BREED)—to mate and raise a certain kind of animal

camouflage (KA-muh-flazh)—a pattern or color on an animal's skin that helps it blend in with the things around it

cold-blooded (KOHLD-BLUHD-id)—having a body temperature that changes with the surrounding temperature

dune (DOON)—a hill or ridge of sand piled up by the wind

habitat (HAB-uh-tat)—the natural place and conditions in which a plant or animal lives

hatchling (HACH-ling)—a young animal that has just come out of its egg

mammal (MAM-uhl)—a warm-blooded animal that breathes air; mammals have hair or fur; female mammals feed milk to their young

mate (MAYT)—to join with another to produce young

molt (MOHLT)—to shed an outer layer of skin

nocturnal (nok-TUR-nuhl)—active at night and resting during the day

predator (PRED-uh-tur)—an animal that hunts other animals for food

prey (PRAY)—an animal hunted by another animal for food

reptile (REP-tile)—a cold-blooded animal that breathes air and has a backbone; most reptiles have scales

species (SPEE-sheez)—a group of animals with similar features

Read More

Craats, Rennay. *Gecko*. My Pet. New York: Weigl Publishers, 2010.

Hernandez-Divers, Sonia. *Geckos*. Keeping Unusual Pets. Chicago: Heinemann Library, 2010.

Silverman, Buffy. *Can You Tell a Gecko from a Salamander?* Lightning Bolt Books: Animal Look-alikes. Minneapolis: Lerner, 2012.

Internet Sites

FactHound offers a safe, fun way to find Internet sites related to this book. All of the sites on FactHound have been researched by our staff.

Here's all you do:
Visit *www.facthound.com*
Type in this code: 9781491420607

Check out projects, games and lots more at
www.capstonekids.com

Critical Thinking Using the Common Core

1. How do geckos use their sounds to survive in the wild? (Key Ideas and Details)

2. Think about how your body has special parts to help you do different jobs. What parts of a gecko's body help it survive in its environment? How? (Integration of Knowledge and Ideas)

Index

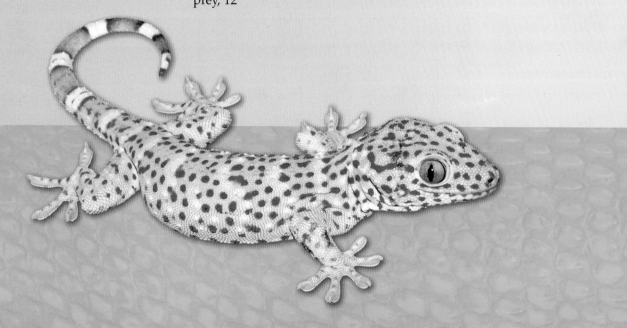